Then *&* Now
HARROGATE

Montpelier Gardens, on a sunny spring morning. Just beyond the trees is Parliament Street, with the Cenotaph, St Peter's church and the Prospect Hotel just visible.
(25 April '98)

Then & Now
HARROGATE

Compiled by
David J. Jenkinson

TEMPUS

First published 1998
Copyright © David J. Jenkinson, 1998

Tempus Publishing Limited
The Mill, Brimscombe Port,
Stroud, Gloucestershire, GL5 2QG

ISBN 0 7524 1502 6

Typesetting and origination by
Tempus Publishing Limited
Printed in Great Britain by
Midway Clark Printing, Wiltshire

Contents

Acknowledgements

I would like to extend my sincerest thanks to North Yorkshire County Council and the staff at Harrogate library, Mr Clifford Hopes, Mr David Beeken, Miss Fiona Movley, Mr G.C. East and Mr W. Martin for the 'Then' photographs in this study. John Wilson at Stray FM's Actionline, Jim Jack at *The Harrogate Advertiser* and Harrogate Photographic Laboratories for their kind assistance. Nidd Vale Motors, Barry Blades Florist, the staff and manager of the Halifax bank (Oxford Street), D. Stalker, The Academy and Harlow Carr Botanical Gardens for their assistance in letting me intrude on their property. Thanks also to everybody who has called with photographs and stories.

A special thanks goes to my dad, Roy Jenkinson, for so effectively proof reading the text and for being my chief critic. Also to Fiona Movley who, as well as supplying a number of old photographs, went out of her way to be of assistance to me in the latter stages of this book.

Introduction

It is not difficult to picture how Harrogate must have looked in its earliest form. One has merely to venture out into the dales to see the countless small villages that litter the open countryside, surrounded by stone walls, to gain an idea of the two antediluvian villages of High and Low Harrogate, with neighbouring Bilton and Starbeck, nestling in the ancient Forest of Knaresborough. This, until the eighteenth century at least, was Harrogate.

Then it all changed. The great Award of 1778 served to protect the Wells, establish the Stray and lay the foundation for the future of Harrogate. The next two centuries saw the development of the town through a whole host of stages, with the town centred on its Spa and Stray.

Thus, Harrogate became what it is today - a centre for business and the conference industry. Harrogate is a live display of a cross-section of history, encompassing a wide variety of architectural styles, from the Victorian crescents to the eighties' conference centre.

I need not venture too deeply into the history of the town here. Any number of superb publications serve that purpose. Here we will instead take a look at the changes in Harrogate that have occurred since we started recording the town on film. Changes that have happened slowly and progressively, hardly visible to the naked eye. Changes that individually are perhaps not noticeable, but gathered collectively present a dramatic transformation. Changes which, when presented in the form of 'Then and Now' photographs, become only too obvious.

From a 'Then and Now' perspective Harrogate, on the surface at least, seems to have changed relatively little, the architecture and layout of the town is much as it was a century ago. However, take a closer look. In fact, the town centre has changed dramatically, even over the last decade of the twentieth century, with the construction of the Victoria Gardens shopping centre. Retreat a little further in time and Station Square loses the monstrous Coptall Tower. The railway station becomes, once more, an attractive building. The unsightly, and very controversial, bus station site is again a row of picturesque railway cottages. The list goes on. We discover that ancient building after ancient building has been destroyed to make room for modern structures.

Harrogate, though, is unique in a number of ways. The way the modern buildings are concealed is one example. Walking around the town centre one hardly notices the square, utilitarian structures that have been rammed unceremoniously in between the older, more attractive ones. Don't be mistaken, however, this is not a conscious effort in many instances.

Perhaps we should not criticise the modern buildings. Although they may not fit into the scene created by the developers of the nineteenth century, they are still a part of the town. These buildings illustrate a period in architectural history in the same way as any church or

Victorian crescent. One wonders how many people watched the housing estates of the last century encroach onto surrounding farm land and uttered words of anxiety at what was going on before them! How many people remarked that those buildings didn't 'fit in'?

The buildings are not the only things to have changed. The visitors who once flocked to Harrogate to sample the waters and enjoy the delightful walks through the Valley Gardens are now more likely to be attending the annual toy fair or one of the many conferences held in the town. No longer do ladies promenade the avenues in their finest clothes, shaded by parasols. Now it is the hurried march of commerce, the business suit and mobile telephone that reign supreme. Tourists, of course, do still come to Harrogate. I remember talking to a man in a pub in Lulworth, Dorset, whose face lit up when I mentioned Harrogate. 'My wife and I use it every winter as base for walking the dales' he proudly informed me. A twenty minute walk from the town, in any direction, will take you into the countryside - with no dreary suburbs to trudge through on the way. That must be unique!

Harrogate has taken on a similar form to that of many other large towns and cities. The centre of the town is now almost fully given over to the needs of the shopper. The site occupied by the Market Hall is now The Victoria shopping centre, although the lower floor is still known as the Market Hall and is dedicated to independent traders. The site once occupied by St Peters School, on Cambridge Road, was developed as early as 1937. The school had been demolished to make way for the Regal cinema and a row of shops. These in turn were removed in the early 1980s and a larger development of shops and business premises built.

Meanwhile, the outer regions of Harrogate were developed. Farmland has been swallowed up by housing developments: Jennyfields to the north of the town, Oatlands and Rossett Green to the south and Woodlands to the east - all of these are post war developments. The town has grown rapidly, new communities have formed, each with their own shops and pubs as a focus for the residents. The last fifteen years of the twentieth century have seen Harrogate succumb to the trend of businesses moving to 'out of town' locations. Business parks have either been built from scratch on farmland, Cardale Park on Otley Road for example, or, as in the case of the former ICI Fibres at Hookstone Chase, have been developed and enlarged to suit the needs of the modern business community.

New business has in turn brought about a need for more housing, extending the outlying regions of the town even more. While this is good for the town in many respects, it does have adverse effects. Harrogate still lacks a decent bypass to carry traffic north and south around the town. A bypass, opened in 1992, that links the A658 Bradford road with the A59 York road, effectively carries traffic east to west. However, due to various preservation campaigns, the road was never extended northwards. Therefore, the bottleneck of traffic, which is Harrogate, waits in vain to be relieved. Add to this the shear amount of parking places needed in the town centre, coupled with heavy goods vehicles delivering to shops, and you have all the ingredients for a constant barrage of vehicles from dawn until dusk. This fact becomes apparent from the 'Now' photographs, even though I have made every effort to capture the streets when the traffic is at a minimum.

Yet peel back all of this, remove the hustle and bustle of a modern day city, and one can still stand and imagine the Victorian splendour of the town. The tree-lined avenues are still very much extant, as are the grand villas overlooking parkland, the Spa and the Stray.

Harrogate was always a showpiece town, a picture postcard sort of a place. Even though different architects have had, and will no doubt continue to have, their own ideas of how the town should progress, Harrogate will always retain its unique image.

David J Jenkinson
Knaresborough, April 1998

One
Into Harrogate

A tranquil Leeds Road sees the passing of a steam omnibus, probably from Pannal, and a horse-drawn carriage, c. 1900. The Leeds-Harrogate road was improved as the result of an act of parliament and a turnpike constructed by Knaresborough road builder John Metcalfe, otherwise known as Blind Jack. The continuing improvements demanded by road users are evident here with the road surface, pavements and avenue of recently planted trees.

Not so tranquil today. The A61 Leeds road is a continuous stream of vehicles in both directions. The trees have grown somewhat over the intervening century, but the houses remain little changed. The noise and choking fumes make any time spent time near these busy roads extremely unpleasant. The traffic problem is soon to be compounded by the impending road works, indicated by the sign lying on the road side. (6 April '98)

10

The Prince of Wales Hotel, formerly the Brunswick, occupied a site on the junction of the Harrogate-Leeds and Harrogate-York roads. That particular site had been home to a hotel since Hattersley's opened there in the early nineteenth century. This is a quiet, tree-lined West Park, in 1920, with the occasional shopper and a solitary motor car disappearing into the distance.

In the 1950s The Prince of Wales Hotel became The Prince of Wales Mansions and remains so today. The Prince of Wales roundabout now marks the junction of the Harrogate-Leeds road (the A61) and the Harrogate-York road (the A59). The lone motor car from 1920 has been replaced by a continuous torrent of traffic from all directions. (7 March '98)

WEST PARK HARROGATE　　　　30

The so-called 'roaring twenties' are drawing to a close and Harrogate is in its fashionable heyday in this 1929 view. Despite this, it retains the air of a quiet country town with pleasant walks and interesting shops. The shape of things to come is all too evident though, with the convoy of motor cars making their way to the town.

It seems amazing that, as the twentieth century draws to a close, Harrogate still has to endure a barrage of vehicles along its shopping streets. West Park takes on a cosmopolitan feel in the summer with tables and chairs outside its many pubs. The Stray has a wonderful air about it on a summer evening…in between the lorries, vans and cars. (6 April '98)

The beginning of the end? Moves to widen West Park (seen here in December 1929), by realigning the footpath and encroaching onto the Stray, encountered little opposition in the latter years of the 1920s and early 1930s, although the large flower beds, planted to accompany the newly laid road, were fiercely contested and finally removed in 1933.

The widened West Park is now lined along both sides by parked cars. Even the forward thinkers who sanctioned the widening of the road could not have begun to imagine what an impact the motor car would have on the town sixty or so years later. Today Harrogate suffers from a lack of decent parking facilities, a problem compounded by the introduction of an expensive pay and display scheme in the town centre. (6 April '98)

Ripon Road, Harrogate.

Approaching from the other side of town, *c.* 1928, the Ripon Road undulates down a steep hill from Killinghall to Knox Lane. It rises up again as it approaches New Park, then down to the crossroads with the Skipton Road and then up and over Kent and Duchy Road areas until finally it drops towards the junction with Kings Road. Once again the summer months of the late '20s saw an influx of motor transport.

The wide pavements, which were once a prominent feature of Harrogate, have been truncated to allow widening of the road. This view, from the gateway to Southlands Nursing Home, is just to the right of the original photographer's position. This location was adopted to avoid the juggernauts - the drivers of which often seem blissfully ignorant of the 30mph speed restriction. The office block visible to the left of Parliament Street is Harrogate House. (6 April '98)

A little further down the hill and a little over twenty years earlier than the previous old photograph, a scene has been captured which is so indicative of Harrogate's past. The coal merchant, on horse-drawn truck, makes his way towards Crescent Road around the front of the George Inn. The people of Harrogate enjoy the almost rural atmosphere of Low Harrogate, in March of 1906. The Kursaal, just three years old, is visible on the extreme left.

Assuming a position outside what is now the Swallow Hotel St George, again a few feet to the right of the original photographer's location, the scene is one of complete contrast. The junction of Parliament Street, Kings Road, Ripon Road and Crescent Road is now controlled by an elaborate system of traffic filters and pedestrian crossings, to ensure the safety of the latter and keep a tight control over the former. (6 April '98)

Just off Ripon Road is Swan Road, which led to this detached portion of the Stray at Well Hill (seen here around the turn of the century), on the corner of Swan Road and Cornwall Road. For many years posts and chains were present to prevent horses and their carriages from trampling the site. The old town hall is just visible on the extreme right and the Swan Hotel is in the distance, with Swan Road almost forming a driveway to its front door.

The posts and chains have gone and Swan Road has fallen victim to the need for parking in the town. The old town hall has served a variety of purposes, including housing a theatre which saw Lily Langtray and Oscar Wilde grace its stage. The building presently accommodates The Mercer Gallery, Harrogate's art gallery. (6 April '98)

From near the junction of Crescent Road and Montpelier Road the double frontage of the George Inn can clearly be seen, opposite the Cheltenham Spa Rooms. To the left of The Spa Rooms is the glazed extension of 1871, which was designed by Harrogate architect, Arthur Bown.

The Swallow Hotel St George now faces the Royal Hall, part of the Exhibition and Conference Centre. The Spa Rooms were demolished in 1939 and gardens created on the site. These gardens were later removed to make way for a parking area. The columns from the frontage now form what is known as The Folly, at Harlow Carr Botanical Gardens. At the time of writing the possibility of returning the columns to the site, to form part of a new exhibition hall, is under discussion. (3 April '98)

17

Approaching the town from Wetherby a visitor to Harrogate would eventually pass Devonshire Place. Devonshire Place and Regent Parade, opposite, owe their origins to the old village of High Harrogate. The County Hotel, for many years a resting place for weary travellers, is clearly visible through the gap in the trees, here in the spring of 1937.

The Tetley Pub Company still own and run The County, which today is the 'local' for many residents of High Harrogate. The position adopted by the original photographer is now a bus stop on the busy A59, a road that, like most others in Harrogate, has to bear a relentless flow of vehicles throughout the day. (6 April '98)

Two
Kings Road

Kings Road forms a link from the present day Skipton Road, the main thoroughfare of High Harrogate, to the centre of Low Harrogate at the junction with the Ripon turnpike road. This 1903 view of the then Walker Road, looking towards Skipton Road from the junction with the modern day De Ferriers Avenue, shows the interesting range of small shops that lined this quiet street.

From the same vantage point today, Kings Road, like many of the roads in the town, is lined with parked cars. The Honda dealership on the corner has replaced the row of mock-Tudor style shops, although their neighbour, just beyond, remains intact. (7 April '98)

A little further along Walker Road in the direction of Low Harrogate, but still looking towards Skipton Road, the shops have given way to a peaceful, tree-lined residential area. Once more, an atmospheric view of a long lost Harrogate has been captured here, c. 1900.

Gone is the tranquility! The majority of the houses along this part of Kings Road are now small hotels and guest houses, opened to cater for the influx of people using the Conference Centre just behind the camera. The position is again slightly different (to the left), a necessity to avoid the traffic. The tree on the extreme left is the same one seen in the original picture. (7 April '98)

Ash Grove, situated between Strawberry Dale Avenue and Alexandra Road was numbered 48 to 74 Kings Road and 14 Strawberry Dale Avenue. This was considered to be one of the most peaceful parts of Harrogate, facing as it did the wooded gardens behind the Spa Rooms. Here though, around 1925, the shape of things to come is apparent, as a delivery van and private motor car make their way along the renamed now Kings Road.

From directly outside the entrance to the Conference Centre the junction with Strawberry Dale Avenue sees a constant flow of vehicles, interrupted only by the pedestrian crossing just visible in the top left hand corner. The horse chestnut tree visible in the original photograph has long since vanished – it and its surroundings replaced by the red-brick and mirrored-glass Conference Centre. (7 April '98)

The houses have once more given way to shops as Walker Road reaches Low Harrogate, c. 1910. On the left are the railings surrounding the Spa Rooms Gardens. The gardens lay in the shelter of a continuing avenue of trees that lined the road throughout the first half of the twentieth century.

Our first view of the Conference Centre, in all its (questionable) glory, which towers over Low Harrogate. Of typical eighties design, one wonders whether such a development would be permitted today – it forms such a stark contrast to the rest of this area of Harrogate. The trees, like so many in the town, have long since succumbed to the saw and the gardens, which once extended over six acres, have been swallowed up by exhibition halls and a car park. (7 April '98)

This is Crescent Road, included here to show its proximity to Kings Road. The building pictured, possibly around 1880, was the old Montpelier Baths. As well as the baths this building housed the bottling depot that bottled the waters for sale.

The Royal Baths were opened in 1897 by the Duke of Cambridge, who lends his name to many of the streets in Harrogate. The building was designed by Baggalley and Bristowe of London as part of a national competition held by Harrogate Council. The baths were considered in their day to be the most advanced centre for hydrotherapy in the world. (3 April '98)

Three
Along Station Parade

Cheltenham Parade, built as one of the Victoria Park Company's residential developments, was the last road to join Walker Road (later Kings Road) with Station Parade, seen here *c.* 1910. The Victoria Park Company intended the properties to be comfortable, middle class houses, forming another tree-lined avenue of the sort that was rapidly becoming the hallmark of Victorian residential Harrogate.

Cheltenham Parade now boasts a variety of interesting shops, but due to the fact that the street is part of the A61 Thirsk to Leeds road, it endures a ceaseless flow of vehicles. The shadow cast across the buildings is that of Harrogate Theatre, the awning of which can be seen at the top of the original photograph. (17 March '98)

Pictured, around the turn of the century, from the junction of Cheltenham Parade and Station Parade, are Station Cottages, built by the North Eastern Railway Company in 1861. After the railway finally arrived in the centre of Harrogate, Station Parade became a focal point for the town centre and was chosen as the location for a wide variety of businesses.

The increasing volume of traffic through the centre of town, along with the demand for better and more frequent local public transport to the outlying regions, finally led to the demolition of Station Cottages in May 1937. The site is now home to the much disputed bus station, which is overshadowed by the Victoria Car Park. Of interest is the manhole cover at the bottom right, still in evidence after one hundred years. Don't be deceived by the apparent lack of traffic, the Jack Russell would have no chance standing here today! (17 March '98)

Howdens, 'The most complete northern motor service', together with a whole host of other small businesses, occupied a row of shops on Station Parade and Station Square that pre-dated many of the other buildings on the street. The Station Hotel, on the left, was at this time still the most prominent building on Station Parade. We see the area in May 1950, shortly before Station Square was enlarged through the demolition of this row.

Victoria Gardens was enlarged in typical '50s style after the demolition of Howdens, but by 1990 had developed a scruffy appearance. During the demolition of the market hall and subsequent construction of The Victoria Gardens Centre, pictured here, Victoria Gardens was used as accommodation for a temporary market hall. The site was redesigned and reinstated shortly thereafter. (18 March '98)

Station Square, looking towards James Street from within the Station Gardens, on a bright, spring morning, c. 1905. On the corner of Station Square and James Street are the premises of Edward Standing, family grocer and café. Standings first opened in 1882, boasting a smokeroom, grocery, café and bakery. The shop was refurbished in 1919 and finally closed down in its 100th year, 1982.

The premises on the corner of Station Square and James Street after another refurbishment. The shuttering has just come down to reveal Gap, a clothes store. The crescent-shaped colonnade frontage of The Victoria Gardens Centre is visible just beyond the Victoria or Jubilee Monument. The edifice on the right is part of Thomas' Bar, which in turn is part of the Coptall Tower development. (18 March '98)

Looking north along Station Parade, in 1911. The centre of Harrogate has a cosmopolitan air about it in the optimistic early years of the reign of King George V. The horse-drawn taxis wait for custom outside the railway station, all under the watchful eye of Queen Victoria.

Queen Victoria now stands in the shadow of the Coptall Tower that dominates Harrogate's skyline. Station Parade seems quiet on this Wednesday morning, but don't be deceived, the traffic lights at the far end of the road were working in my favour. (18 March '98)

The very top end of Station Parade is pictured in December 1930, shortly before the construction of the Spa Garage. On the right hand side of the street are the properties designed by Arthur Bown for the Victoria Park Company. Of interest are the 'figure of eight' railings visible along both sides of the street, these were a trademark of the Victoria Park Company and could be seen all across their estates.

The railings were lost during the salvage programme initiated for the war effort. The site once occupied by the piano manufacturers is now the Safeway food store. Station Parade has yet to fill up with parked cars on this particular day, but it is early yet. (8 April '98)

The first of two views of 'Holyrood', c. 1936. This was another product of Arthur Bown and the Victoria Park Company. The house stood in large gardens on the corner of Station Parade and Victoria Avenue and occupied all the grounds between the road and railway.

An uninspiring view of a road sign and Safeways' far from picturesque car park. A far cry from 'Holyrood' and Arthur Bown's idea of Harrogate, this reflects perfectly the shifting of roles of the different areas. The residential Harrogate, with a few exceptions, has moved to the suburbs, while more room has been made in the town centre for businesses of all descriptions. (8 April '98)

Looking north once more, the extent of the grounds belonging to 'Holyrood' can be made out. The majority of the grounds were swallowed up as Spa Garage encroached onto the site between the end of the Second World War and the early 1980s.

Some of the original boundary wall is still extant at the junction with Victoria Avenue, albeit in truncated form, surrounding the remaining villa. The premises are now used as a solicitors office. Spa Garage was demolished in the early 1980s and Safeways was erected soon afterwards. In order to reclaim land to build a car park, Safeways built a 'raft' over the railway, creating almost a tunnel as you leave Harrogate station. (8 April '98)

Just off Station Parade is Raglan Street, which runs parallel with Victoria Avenue. This building, seen in 1897, was possibly a social hall. It was removed to a site on Skipton Road where, at the time of writing, it is still in use.

Henry Hare's plans for a spectacular Municipal Palace, on the corner of Victoria Avenue and Station Parade were never fully realised. Only the end of the Victoria Avenue wing was completed, to be used as the town's library. The quoin stones still jut out from the walls of the library ready to attach to the remainder of the building, which would have stood in what is now the library gardens. (3 April '98)

Station bridge leads away from Station Parade, almost opposite Raglan Street, to a part of Harrogate that evolved around the railway in the town. For many years Harrogate's sorting office was situated just around the corner from here, opposite the back of the railway station. The roof line of the Station Hotel is visible above the signal box, illustrating how open Station Square was prior to the 1960s.

My favourite of all Harrogate's 'Then and Now' images. The left hand, or southern side of Station Bridge is little changed, while opposite, Station Square has been ravaged by the intrusion of the Coptall Tower and its associated development. This view is from the roundabout outside the Odeon cinema. (7 March '98)

A few yards to the north and facing in the opposite direction in the mid-1930s, this is the site purchased for the Odeon cinema. To the left is the roof of the old sorting office. Beyond that is Arthington Avenue, dating from the 1920s.

The Odeon opened its doors in 1937 and has outlived all of Harrogate's other cinemas. The sorting office was demolished in 1991 and replaced with a development of retirement apartments. Beyond the cinema, on the remainder of the field visible in the original shot, is yet another car park. Arthington Avenue is much the same as it was. (19 March '98)

Four
Parliament Street

STRAY AND CONGREGATIONAL CHURCH, HARROGATE

The Stray and Congregational church, pictured from Beech Grove, *c*. 1930. The church was built by Lockwood and Mawson during 1861 and '62. It is prominently situated on the corner of West Park, before it becomes Parliament Street, and the then new Victoria Avenue. The building shows striking similarities to the Baptist church located on Victoria Circus, a little further back along Victoria Avenue.

From outside Stray House, a development of luxury apartments dating from the early 1970s, the view along Beech Grove towards West Park and Victoria Avenue is little changed. Those trees that remain now obscure the church, while more of the buildings on West Park are visible where some trees have been lost. (8 April '98)

Parliament Street, seen in 1911, has been a focus for the people of Harrogate since its serious development by George Dawson, in the early 1860s. The Café Imperial, which is now Betty's, was built around 1900. The wall on the extreme right enclosed the Prospect Hotel tennis courts and gardens.

The demands of Harrogate traffic dictate that Parliament Street is still a busy place today. The Prospect Hotel's gardens were reclaimed by the town after the First World War for the construction of Harrogate's war memorial, today known as the Cenotaph. The pavement was moved to allow widening of the road, and today is set well back, giving some respite to the weary pedestrian. (3 April '98)

George Dawson's contribution to Parliament Street is shown to good effect here, c. 1925. The row of buildings second from the right, with the pagoda-style second floor windows, was built during the years 1866 to '68. During this time, Dawson began construction of the much larger Cambridge Crescent, on the extreme right, which effectively took Parliament Street around into the new and rapidly expanding town centre.

It was not possible to achieve the height of the earlier photographer's position due to the nature of the road. A few steps back and a slight extension to the left and right hopefully gives a just illustration of the view north along Parliament Street today. (8 April '98)

The premises of W.H. Smith and Son, 'successors to Ainsworths' as the shop sign informs us, as it appeared on the left side of a panoramic post card dating from 1905, at 18 Parliament Street. Chapel Street disappears off to the left. Chapel Street joined up with Parliament Street about halfway down the hill into the centre of Low Harrogate.

W.H. Smith occupied the building on the corner of Parliament Street and the renamed Oxford Street, albeit in a drastically altered form, until 1997, when they moved to the Victoria Gardens Centre. The building is now home to Lloyds No1, a bar and restaurant. (8 April '98)

Two views of St Peter's School, shortly before its demolition, taken from the top and bottom of Cambridge Road respectively, in 1936. The school was built in 1865, but by the thirties the shift of residential areas towards the outskirts of the town, and the demand for more town centre business space, struck the final blow for the school.

After St Peter's School came the Regal cinema in 1937. This in turn was demolished in the early 1980s. This row, incorporating a variety of different businesses, was built on the vacant site and has frontages onto both Cambridge Road and Oxford Street. (18 March '98)

These photographs show the demolition of St Peter's School. These were taken shortly after the preceding set, towards the end of the summer of 1936. The school was razed to the ground and the site cleared over a period of three weeks, by a local contractor.

Two views of the development of shops and businesses that succeeded the Regal cinema in 1984. The building, known as Nidderdale House, is one of the first examples of 'sympathetic' design in the town, and it can surely only be seen as an improvement on the architectural style of the Regal. The picture below was taken from the upper floor of the present day Halifax bank building. (18 March '98)

'This is a real photograph' proudly states the back of this 1950s picture postcard view of Cambridge Crescent, The Cenotaph and St Peter's church. Beyond St Peter's, in the centre, is the Regal. Photographs of the Regal are rare, Clarrie East, who provided this picture, was married at St Peter's and told me that his wedding photographs all had the Regal as their backdrop.

Spring sunshine bathes Harrogate town centre as the borough council gardeners tidy the gardens outside the Prospect Hotel. Very little seems to have changed, save the street signs and cars. (8 April '98)

Cambridge Street, seen here in July 1928, is known to many residents of Harrogate as 'the main drag'. It has, together with James Street, established itself as Harrogate's main shopping area. For many years it was the home of the market hall. The Scala, Harrogate's first purpose-built cinema, opened in 1920 on land formerly occupied by the stables of the Prospect Hotel. The shadow in the foreground is that of St Peter's church.

After the demolition of the Scala's later incarnation, the Gaumont, in 1961, this mundane building (housing Littlewoods) was erected. The market hall was destroyed by fire in 1937 and its replacement was itself replaced in 1991 with The Victoria Gardens Shopping Centre. (7 March '98)

Prior to the construction of the Scala Super Cinema, this small picture house faced Cambridge Street. It is seen here *c.* 1919. Near this site were the premises of B. Wardman, engineers. During the First World War Wardman built aircraft wings for A.V. Roe (AVRO) Ltd.

The Scala's replacement building, a Littlewoods store, sits unceremoniously between two much grander properties. The building has a typically 1960s utilitarian look, and overshadows its Victorian neighbour to the left. (3 April '98)

Five

Harrogate Railway Station

The lower Crimple viaduct as it looked shortly after the lifting of the tracks, August 1951. The second of the two railway companies to reach Harrogate was the Leeds and Thirsk, later the Leeds Northern, who opened their station in Starbeck on 1 September 1848. In the distance is the upper Crimple viaduct, built by the York and North Midland company to access their Brunswick railway station.

The viaduct is now fenced off and signed as being a dangerous structure. As is usually the case somebody has cut a hole in the wire to allow access over the structure. The upper Crimple viaduct still carries trains into Harrogate every thirty minutes. (19 March '98)

Turning to face in the other direction, towards Harrogate, Jimmy Hague (who took all the 'then' photographs in this chapter) has captured the course of the former Leeds Northern as it passed The Yorkshire Showground, again in August 1951. The chimney in the distance is that of the former brick works that stood on Wetherby Road.

The course of the line has been bulldozed and incorporated into the outer regions of the showground. On the right are the remnants of the building materials used to extend the showground's buildings during 1996. The bare soil exposed after the removal of the ballast in 1951 has given way to a concrete road laid in November 1951. (19 March '98)

A short distance further on, still in August 1951, and the brickworks chimney becomes clearer, as does the bridge carrying Wetherby Road. The infill, just to this side of the bridge, is the access constructed by contractors to facilitate easy removal of the line. A sad image for any railway enthusiast

Lying flat on what is now Railway Road, a road leading to Sainsbury's supermarket and the showground, I was still ten feet or so too high to capture the exact angle of the earlier picture. The bridge that once spanned the line has long since gone to allow widening of the road. The junction now marks the site. Beyond is a monumental mason's premises. (19 March '98)

In July 1953, Jimmy Hague captured a class B16 locomotive passing Dragon Junction on its approach to Harrogate Station. The line north to Ripon curves to the left behind the locomotive, while the branch line to York curves to the right. The line just behind the locomotive serviced a factory.

The footbridge was replaced during the 1960s, shortly before the line to Ripon was closed on 5 March 1967. The branch line to York then became the main line. The Claro Road Business Park, built on the site of the factory, is just visible in the distance underneath the bridge. (19 March '98)

A J39 and Austerity enter Harrogate station from the north, in June 1951. Beyond the train is the expanse of the Strawberry Dale, Franklin and Kings Road developments. The spire of St Lukes church on Kings Road can be seen above the tender of the leading locomotive. Harrogate's goods facilities dwindled after the war, to a point where freight services merely passed through before ceasing altogether in the 1970s.

From a slightly different location, just forward of Mr Hague's because of a small storage shed, the railway takes on a bleak appearance on the approach to the station. The skyline north over Harrogate is little changed. St Lukes, which became redundant in 1979, has since been converted into twenty-nine apartments. (18 March '98)

In the early 1930s the extent of the railway activities in Harrogate can be seen, these include the extensive motive power depot just behind the locomotive tender. Harrogate's new north signal box has yet to be built. Beyond the front of the locomotive is the southernmost extremity of the Dragon Estate of the 1860s.

A good example of the track rationalisation that was the trademark of British Railways during the post war years. Harrogate's motive power depot is now an Asda superstore, the only superstore left in the centre of the town. The signal box is of a typically austere design so common on the LNER between the wars. The corner of the storage shed mentioned previously can be seen on the far right of the picture. (18 March '98)

The 12.55 passenger working from Northallerton, behind *The Morpeth*, draws into platform 2 at Harrogate, on 2 June 1951. The extent of the platform canopies, together with the Victorian footbridge, can be clearly appreciated in this view. Just beyond the lead locomotive, carriages can be seen in Harrogate's bay platform. The houses beyond the station are those opposite the sorting office on East Parade.

Taken from against the wall of the basement car park belonging to the Coptall Tower, the restored platforms and new footbridges at Harrogate can be clearly seen. The 1992 Victoria car park towers over the station. With the canopies removed the houses on East Parade are even more evident. The bay platform was removed some years ago and infilled to form a car park. (18 March '98)

By the early 1950s, Harrogate station is starting to look slightly run down. A grimy B16 brings a passenger service from Northallerton to a halt at platform 2.

After too many years of apparent neglect, Harrogate station has undergone a partial facelift since 1992. The footbridge, Victorian in origin, was replaced when the Victoria car park was built, followed by a gradual improvement programme. Since the station became the property of RailTrack, the platforms have undergone complete restoration, having been resurfaced and had new edging constructed. (18 March '98)

Six

Streets Around Town

Seen from the corner of Skipton Road and Grove Road, these cottages were situated in the area known as Smithy Hill. The building beyond the premises of G. Inman, with the arched window and apex visible, was St Luke's institute, the first home of Harrogate Boys Club.

All the buildings in the original photograph were razed to the ground between the wars. Skipton Road, now the main A59, has been widened to meet the demands of the motorist and now suffers an endless barrage from traffic passing through the town. The building in the foreground belongs to North Yorkshire County Council, the one in background is Harrogate fire station. (7 March '98)

A short distance along Skipton Road, on the junction with Chatsworth Road, F. Clarke, family grocer had his shop, pictured here in 1938. The shop doubled up as Skipton Road post office. For many years this row looked out over open fields which stretched out north of Harrogate. Advertisements adorning the building were a familiar sight of this period.

The cottages on Chatsworth Road, part of the so-called Smithy Hill Clearance Area, were demolished during the 1950s and replaced by the apartments just visible. F. Clarke's premises, most recently accommodating a double glazing showroom, have now stood empty for some time. The post box is still in service, but has been moved just around the corner onto Chatsworth Road. (14 April '98)

Returning to the centre of town. James Street is shown, by 1930, to be rapidly developing as a focal point for the businesses of Harrogate. This busy scene demonstrates just how thriving Harrogate had become, with the routine of daily life beginning to pick up a momentum that would continue into the present day.

James Street is now infamous for being a bottleneck across the centre of town. Both sides of the now one-way street are lined with parked cars, while pedestrians and motorists fight for space in this busy shopping area. It seems a pity that Cambridge Street and its surrounding area have been pedestrianised, forming a haven for shoppers, while the equally important James Street has been left to the ravages of the car and lorry. (14 April '98)

Once again in 1930, James Street is seen here from Station Parade and the famous Standings Café. This would have been the first view of Harrogate that many travellers would see on leaving the railway station. J.H. Hirst, who designed the eastern end of James Street, intended it to be an imposing first glimpse of the town. The land, together with many other parts of Harrogate, was donated by Richard Ellis.

Trying to judge the traffic on Station Parade is a skill in itself, and one that had to be quickly mastered in order to achieve this shot from the opposite side of the street. James Street seems to have changed relatively little from an architectural point of view and still forms an impressive welcome to the town for rail travellers, despite the exhaust fumes! (14 April '98)

This building, seen in the mid-1930s, formed part of J.H. Hirst's development of 1865 and took James Street around into Princess Street. The awning just visible on the left is that of Marshall and Snelgrove, the pioneering department store that for many years, together with its commissionaire, was a landmark of James Street.

One of the later residents of the building, The Yorkshire Penny Bank, has expanded somewhat over the years and now occupies the entire site. Hirst's 1865 building was unceremoniously redeveloped in the early 1950s to accommodate The Yorkshire Bank, its new façade forming a utilitarian contrast to its ornate predecessor. One of Harrogate's CCTV columns can be seen just in front of the building. (8 April '98)

In the middle of the junction with Kings Road, in 1922, this is Harrogate as it was destined to become. The variety of shops that was to become a trademark of the town is shown to good effect here, as Harrogate begins its transition into a modern shopping town. The building on the left is the manager's house which abutted the Cheltenham Spa Rooms.

The building second from the right, an opticians premises in the original picture, is now a pub and nightclub that extends over three floors. The car park built on the site of the Spa Rooms is clearly visible on the left. (7 April '98)

Princes Square as its designers intended it to look. At this time, 1929, Princes Square was still a quiet side street tucked away from the hustle and bustle of the town centre. The impressive residences have still to be converted into offices, but that time is not far distant, as can be judged by the premises of Day and Son and the Bingley Building Society.

The railings were removed and the road widened shortly after the date of the original photograph. Most of the buildings now accommodate either estate agents or solicitors offices, overlooking another clogged up area of Harrogate. It seems that every available space has to be used by the town to meet parking needs, although Princes Square is not as popular for parking as it once was due to the fact it is now part of the pay and display scheme. (14 April '98)

MONTPELLIAR PARADE, HARROGATE.

12

Montpelier Parade in its pseudo-rural setting, overlooking the northernmost part of the Stray, in 1933. The carriages lining the street were a feature of the area for many years and tours could be taken throughout the year to enjoy the splendours of the town.

Montpelier Parade still has a cosmopolitan air about it. During the summer months, the Stray here is alive with people enjoying the country atmosphere and diverse range of shops so close to the town centre. The shelters, originally provided for the carriage drivers, still remain.
(25 April '98)

Benwell House occupied an impressive site on Well Hill, close to the Valley Gardens. As it became increasingly obvious that the need for improved roads far outweighed housing demands in this area, it was decided to remove Benwell House. This photograph, taken during the course of demolition, in 1921, shows other houses that were later to be removed as well, in order to improve the Valley Gardens.

Well Hill is now part of Cornwall Road which leads to the outskirts of the Duchy estate, and out into the countryside near Birk Crag. The Valley Gardens is still as popular as ever, even when April sees snow. The site is currently undergoing a period of restoration, as is evidenced by the scaffolding around the Sun Pavilion, visible in the distance. (14 April '98)

Another link from High Harrogate to Low Harrogate is formed by Westmoreland Street and East Parade, which lead via the Dragon estate to Station Parade. For many years a predominantly residential area, East Parade, together with Dragon Parade, Dragon Avenue and Dragon Road, formed the vast estate which was built on the site of Dragon Farm during the 1860s. The area is pictured here around 1905.

Recently developed as far as High Harrogate goes, this building is promoted by the owners, Nidd Vale Motors, as Yorkshire's biggest indoor car showroom. Westmoreland Street and East Parade have been widened over the years, but are still narrow by today's standards. The two trees just in front of the showroom are two of those visible in the original view. (19 March '98)

Albany Road, pictured *c.* 1930, is part of the enormous estate that grew to the north of Skipton Road between the wars. The houses, built in a back-to-back style, are typical of those built to accommodate the now better off worker that emerged during the 'austerity' years. The car has yet to feature as a part of Albany Road, but it was not far off at this time.

Albany Road now sits quietly within a much larger development, which is essentially an extension of Bilton. The estates which branch out from either side of Woodhead Road take Harrogate to its northernmost extremity, where the houses have come to an abrupt halt by the formation belonging to the former Leeds Northern railway. (16 April '98)

Seven
Buildings Around Town

The Coppice Valley Swimming Pool sits in a hollow just off Springfield Avenue, a street that links Ripon Road to Kings Road. The pool is pictured in April 1966. Harrogate Borough Council began construction of the pool in late summer 1965 and by early summer 1966 the building was nearing completion, with only the fitting out work left to undertake. The pool was officially opened on 31 October 1966.

Thirty-two years on and Coppice Valley Pool nears the end of its working life. A short distance away, at the junction of Ripon Road and Jennyfields Avenue, Harrogate Borough Council are constructing a brand new sports and leisure complex on former playing fields. Coppice will eventually close and, due to the ravages of age on its concrete construction, faces almost certain demolition. (3 April '98)

Among the oldest buildings on Regent Parade was this pair of cottages that stood near the junction with Dragon Parade. Although very little is documented about them, they almost certainly dated from the eighteenth century development of the village of High Harrogate when Regent Parade was known as Paradise Row. The cottages were demolished at the turn of the century.

Park Parade Motors presently occupies the site of the cottages which now overlooks the A59. Beyond the gap created when the cottages were demolished, the rear of properties on Westmoreland Street can be made out, alongside Thompson's Yard, a Victorian courtyard named after a nineteenth-century joiner, William Thompson. (19 March '98)

In the eighteenth century, many commercial establishments were set up in High Harrogate to cater for the increasing number of visitors to the spa. Many of the shops which opened belonged to enterprising Knaresborough traders, who traded only seasonally. In 1775, Harrogate was regarded as a small village, many even thought it not to be as well served as most market towns. By 1822 though, all but three of Harrogate's shops were situated in High Harrogate.

With the shift towards Low Harrogate caused by the opening of the central railway station, most traders removed their premises from High Harrogate and reopened in the rapidly developing new town centre. Here only one of the two shops remains open and the nature of the business reflects the needs of today's shopper. High Harrogate has returned to having the atmosphere of a thriving village, as opposed to being part of a large town. (19 March '98)

The Devonshire Hotel on Devonshire Place overlooks the narrowest part of the Stray, it is seen here *c.* 1910. The hotel was opened in about 1866, but it is known that a Wine and Spirit Merchant and Ale and Porter Brewer occupied the same address prior to this date.

The refurbished Devonshire has fallen victim to the trend of the breweries to give their premises new identities, and since 1996 has been called Molly Malone's. The front door now has to be protected by railings, due to the amount of vehicles using the A59. (19 March '98)

The Northern Police Orphanage, formerly St George's College, in 1900. It was purchased as an orphanage in November 1897 by Catherine Gurney, for the sum of £10,000. The first child, Minnie Smith, was taken in during January 1898, closely followed by two brothers, George and Alexander Nuttall. The house was renamed The Northern Police Orphanage at the first meeting of the General and Finance Committee, a name it carried until 1942.

The Northern Police Orphanage became St George's House in 1942. The building continued in use as an orphanage until dwindling numbers forced the institute to move to smaller premises at 16 Hereford Road in January 1955. This house in turn closed shortly after that, in August 1956. St George's, meanwhile, was demolished after a period of disuse, and Swinton Court, a development of housing for disabled people, was eventually built on the site. (15 April '98)

In the early 1890s Harrogate Corporation became the owner of two public utilities, one of which was electricity. Councillor David Simpson, who built the Duchy Estate, pressed the Corporation to undertake the electricity works itself, and after much debate he succeeded. The works are seen here in August 1922. The municipal electricity works were built on the Corporation's Irrigation Farm and the supply was up and running by April 1897.

By the early 1960s the demand for power in the growing town forced the closure of these works. The electricity board converted the buildings into a depot for tradesmen. Then, when the staff were moved to larger premises, it became a training centre for apprentices. Eventually this in turn was closed, and the site was abandoned altogether. The building was eventually bought by a leisure company and became The Academy, a superbly equipped health and fitness centre. (16 April '98)

Valley Drive runs parallel to, and overlooks, the Valley Gardens. The Valley Gardens were created along the route of an ancient public footpath that crossed land owned by the Vicar of Pannal. The popularity of the gardens led to most of the properties along Valley Drive becoming private hotels and guesthouses. Here, at numbers 13 to 15, is The Octagon, situated on the corner of Valley Road.

HARROGATE - THE OCTAGON.

Valley Drive continues to play host to visitors to Harrogate and just about all of these properties prosper from the influx the town experiences throughout the summer months. Unfortunately Valley Drive has to endure the weight of traffic struggling to pass along its length, hindered by the rows of parked vehicles along both sides.
(16 April '98)

The Royal Bath Hospital, seen here around 1930, dates in its present form from the rebuilding of 1889. It was originally opened in 1824 and was built on land donated by the Earl of Harewood. The hospital was built and run by charitable subscription, giving the poorer members of the community the chance to savour the healing waters of Harrogate, originally a privilege reserved for the wealthy.

This building is now Park House and Kennion House. The Royal Bath Hospital was closed in 1994 and for a time stood empty. The buildings were threatened with demolition because of repeated break-ins and arson attacks, but were saved by Crosby Homes who purchased the former hospital. The site is now Sovereign Park, a development of luxury houses. This photograph is from a slightly different viewpoint in order to gain a view through the builder's shuttering. (15 April '98)

Cold Bath Road, originally known as Robin Hood Lane, was an important location for Coaching Inns, one of which was The Adelphi Hotel. The Adelphi, pictured around 1910, was first known as the Leeds Terrace Boarding House. After being bought by Joshua Bower in 1859, it was enlarged and improved.

The Adelphi was partly demolished in the early 1990s, only the façade on the extreme left remained. Thus it was for a number of years, the listed stone façade held aloft by scaffolding. Eventually, McCarthy Stone acquired the site and the new Adelphi rose Phoenix-like over Cold Bath Road to become retirement apartments. (15 April '98)

Springs of sulphur water were discovered here, on land belonging to the Forest of Knaresborough, in 1734. However, over a hundred years were to pass before any were utilised. Then in 1840 Henry Wright, who owned the estate, cleaned and protected one of the wells. Four years later Mr Wright built a bath house and the Harlow Car Hotel, laying out gardens around the bath house at the same time, it is seen here around 1910. Bathers paid 2s 6d to experience the waters.

The Harlow Car Hotel is now the Harrogate Arms and is quite separate from the rest of what is now Harlow Carr Botanical Gardens. The bath house was converted into a study centre during 1958 and boasts a library, meeting room and offices. Eventually six wells were discovered outside the bath house, all of which were capped. Despite this, the smell of the sulphur, reminiscent of rotten eggs, sometimes pervades the air. (15 April '98)

The Claremont, which stands opposite the Baptist church on Victoria Avenue, was a private hotel, owned for many years by Mrs Gowland. It is pictured here in 1907. Built to complement the existing buildings of the Victoria Park Company, the Claremont had the 'figure of eight' railings, a hallmark of the Victoria Park Company, surrounding its grounds.

The Claremont is now Claremont House, a development of offices. As with all the other properties on Victoria Avenue the railings were lost to the salvage drive initiated during the Second World War. The author wonders how much the former properties of the Victoria Park Company, and indeed Harrogate, would benefit from these railings being replaced. (15 April '98)

From the Low Harrogate end of Parliament Street the George Hotel commands a prominent position on Cheltenham Square in 1905. The hotel opened around 1773 as the George Inn. In 1828 William Barber acquired the property and proceeded to enlarge it. The large extension that fronts onto Crescent Gardens was built during the last half of the nineteenth century.

The busy junction with Ripon Road is a far cry from the serene atmosphere of 1905. Vehicles now bombard this area night and day. As mentioned in chapter one, the George Hotel has become the Swallow Hotel St George, part of Vaux Breweries. It has also had two floors added to its northern-most wing. (16 April '98)

The Station Hotel was built in 1873 to a design by Arthur Hiscoe, it is seen here *c.* 1900. The building was extended during 1890 by Arthur Bown and wound its way around into Albert Street, forming an imposing structure. The buildings at this end of James Street were intended to be some of the finest in Harrogate, they were adorned with a fine variety of ornate dressed stonework.

The Station Hotel became the North Eastern, in honour of the former railway company, before becoming Eddison's in 1996. The upper floors are now office space. (16 April '98)

Harrogate Technical College and Secondary School were built on the corner of East Parade and Bower Road, known as Haywra Crescent, during 1898-99. The building was on the edge of the Dragon estate and was considered to be one of the finest on that estate; it is seen here in 1910.

The buildings were demolished in 1996 after standing empty for over ten years. McCarthy Stone, who have become so prominent in Harrogate, built Haywra Court on the site. It seems such a pity that the original buildings could not have been converted for the purpose, instead of using the so-called sympathetic design of the present building. (15 April '98)

Having been there since 1903, Harrogate Grammar School was well established in the town centre by the early 1930s, but was rapidly outgrowing its accommodation. In the words of the headmaster it was, 'the most unsuitable building of the last 50 years'. In 1933, £100,000 was spent building these premises on Arthur's Avenue, just off Otley Road, seen *c.* 1934. The new building, dubbed the finest in the country, boasted purpose built laboratories, woodwork and metalwork shops.

The school building hides behind a screen of trees and shrubs sixty-four years later. Harrogate Grammar School has established itself as Harrogate's oldest surviving state school. The site has expanded over the years, and can now cater for far more than the 700 pupils originally intended. (15 April '98)

Just as the Second World War was beginning Harrogate Borough Council set about demolishing the Cheltenham Spa Rooms. The site was cleared and eventually laid out as gardens, creating a picturesque boundary to one side of Kings Road.

Not the same location, but the same structure. After the bulk of the material from the Spa Rooms was removed, the columns were placed in pieces in one corner of the Valley Gardens. The sections lay there until the 1960s when it was decided to destroy them. At the eleventh hour, the columns were saved from destruction and presented to the Northern Horticultural Society, who re-erected them as The Folly at Harlow Car Gardens.
(15 April '98)

Eight

Churches

HARROGATE: ST.PAULS PRESBYTERIAN CHURCH

The presbytery of Darlington opened its first preaching station in Harrogate on 9 December 1875. The first minister was inducted shortly afterwards on 24 August 1876, preaching from a temporary 'iron church'. In 1885 construction began on the present building, St Paul's, seen in 1908. The church and hall were finally opened in 1894. St Paul's joined the newly formed presbytery of Yorkshire in 1896.

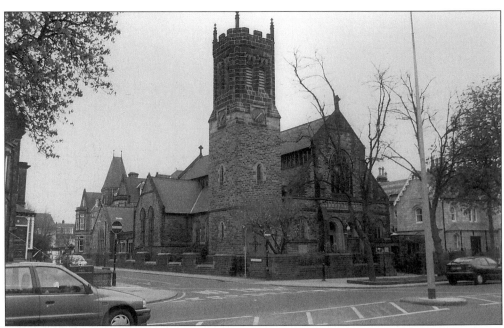

In October 1972 St Paul's became part of the United Reformed Church, joining the National Union of the Presbyterian Church of England and the Congregational Union in England and Wales. The Centenary Rooms were constructed in 1976 to celebrate 100 years of St Paul's. (14 April '98)

Victoria Avenue Congregational Church

Mentioned at the beginning of chapter four, Victoria Avenue Congregational church was built by Lockwood and Mawson during 1861-62. The church occupies a prominent position at the junction of the, then, new Victoria Avenue and West Park. The building, pictured *c.* 1900, could only benefit from being situated on the centre-piece estate of the Victoria Park Company.

From across the road in Victoria Avenue, the United Reformed Methodist church stands overlooking the A61 and Stray. Victoria Avenue is no longer a private thoroughfare and today provides some parking close to the town centre, albeit over priced. (14 April '98)

Harrogate, St. Peter's Church.

The large parish covered by Christ Church, situated on the Stray close to High Harrogate, had become too much for the vicar, the Revd Canon Horatio James, by 1865. As a result, a notice appeared in the *London Gazette* on 14 December 1869 to the effect that a church was to be built on land left by Mary Anne Fielde, after her death on 12 December 1867. The church was designed by J.H. Hirst of Bristol and consecrated by Dr Robert Bickersteth, Lord Bishop of Ripon, on Tuesday 3 October, 1876. The church is pictured in 1912.

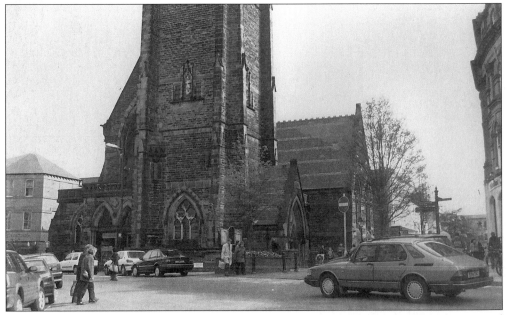

The tower of St Peter's, the lower part of which is just visible behind the tree in the original photograph, was added in 1926 and dedicated on 6 October that year. St Peter's stands like a rose amongst thorns in the middle of Harrogate's main shopping streets. It provides a quiet respite from the hustle and bustle outside. (14 April '98)

Methodist Free Church, & N. E. Hotel, Harrogate.

Across Albert Street, just opposite the Station Hotel, stood the Victoria Park United Methodist Free church, seen *c*. 1890. The church was built in 1865 by Richard Ellis, who donated the land, to a design again by J.H. Hirst. The church had a distinctive short spire, probably intended not to overshadow the town hall planned for, but never built on, adjacent land on Victoria Avenue.

The church, intended to hold 700 worshippers, became redundant after the Second World War and was subsequently bought by the Co-operative Society. In 1953 the church was demolished and replaced by Victoria House, a square, ugly building that was the subject of a feeble face-lift in the mid-1990s. (14 April '98)

Situated in an attractive position in Low Harrogate, St Mary's church, seen here in 1890, gave its name to the street on which it stood, St Mary's Walk. The church, the first in Low Harrogate, was consecrated on 7 August 1825. St Mary's was enlarged in 1865 and was reseated, in 1868, to accommodate 800 worshippers.

St Mary's was declared unsafe in 1904 and, as a result, was disused for a short time. The fabric was eventually removed and used to build a chapel at Harrogate College, now Harrogate Ladies' College, where it still stands. The Pullen family built the cottages that occupy the site today shortly after the church was demolished. (16 April '98)

Twelve years after the first St Mary's church was demolished, Harrogate's second St Mary's, built on Westcliffe Grove, was dedicated. The new St Mary's is seen here in the 1950s. The building was designed by the architect Sir Walter Tapper, consultant architect to York Minster and later surveyor of Westminster Abbey. The church was built at the bequest of Richard Lofthouse, Surgeon General.

The telephone kiosk has moved just around the corner and a number of houses have been built on the extreme left where the gardens once were. Little else seems to have changed, including St Mary's which is partially obscured by trees. (15 April '98)

The recently formed Northern Horticultural Society leased 26 acres of land at Harlow Hill from Harrogate Corporation in 1950 to create Harlow Car Gardens. The intention was to set up a trial ground to test the suitability of plants for growing in northern climates. The guide book for the garden described it as, 'A Wisley of the north'. The man on the right of the three gardeners, seen here in 1951, is Mike Foxon.

Mike Foxon still works at the renamed Harlow Carr Botanical Gardens having done so for much of his working life. The original 26 acres has been expanded to 68 since opening and the investment in facilities has been extensive. In the distance on the extreme right is the visitor's centre, which includes a restaurant, shop and museum, together with a library and study centre housed in the former bath house. (19 March '98)